VIKING TRANMERE

Scandinavian Tranmere
and Wirral

by

Stephen E. Harding

Countyvise Limited, UK

In conjunction with Tranmere Rovers in the Community

First Published 2014 by Countyvise Limited, Wirral, UK.

Copyright © 2014 Stephen E. Harding, University of Nottingham UK.

The right of Stephen E. Harding to be identified as the author of this work has been asserted by him in accordance with the Copyright, Design and Patents Act 1988.

British Library Cataloguing in Publication Data.
A catalogue record for this book is available from the British Library.

Countyvise ISBN 978 1 910352 02 1

Printed by EWS Printers, www.ewsprint.co.uk

Contents

Chapter 1
INTRODUCTION

In or shortly after the year AD 902 a group of Vikings of primarily Norwegian descent led by *Ingimund* came to settle in Wirral after being driven out of Ireland and then Anglesey. This initiated a mass migration of their fellow countrymen into the area and soon they had established a community with their own leader – a man called Ingimund, their own language – Old Norse (perhaps with an Irish accent), a trading port – Meols, and at its centre a place of Assembly or government – the Thing or *Þing* at Thingwall. It would have been during this early settlement period that these Vikings noticed some cranebirds or herons on a sandbank on the banks of the Mersey. Since *trani* is Old Norse for cranebird/heron and mere in this context is from Old Norse *melr* – a sandbank, the word *Tranmelr* – Tranmere, came into being.

A millennium afterwards the connections of Tranmere and Wirral with Norway and Scandinavia are still very strong, particularly in the genes of the people from the area: there is even a "Viking Navy" - and Tranmere Rovers – its football team – preserves this tradition as the only team in the English Football League with a Norse Viking name.

In this short book we will explore this connection, first of all by looking at the arrival of the first Norse settlers and the circumstances surrounding the arrival of Ingimund. We'll look at the settlements as evidenced by all the place name evidence including all the minor place names – with those in Tranmere an excellent example. There is strong evidence for a persistence of a Norse dialect in the area from the minor names, people's names and literature like the well known Sir Gawain and the Green Knight poem: and also the poem's associations with Sir John Stanley of Storeton Hall – which is not far from Prenton Park the home of Tranmere Rovers.

We consider the two Norse ladies of Tranmere – *Gunnhildr* and *Ragnhildr* – and what they may have been like, other Wirral ladies and the Viking men (or men bearing Scandinavian names) of Wirral. Place names and landowner records give over 50 of them, including wonderful names like *Hrafnsvartr* – "the black raven".

Up to 50% of the DNA admixture of old families from Wirral appears to be Norse in origin – not all this necessarily derives from the Viking Period but is nonetheless highly significant. Besides their genes the Norsemen have left behind an impressive array of archaeology including hogback tombstones, fragments of crosses – one of which has been beautifully reconstructed showing the touching image of a Norse couple embracing - and the discovery of what appears to be weaponry from a Viking burial.

Residents of modern Tranmere and Wirral celebrate their Norse heritage with Viking Heritage walks (including St. Olav's Day "mini-pilgrimage") and in supporting Tranmere Rovers. The book closes in considering this football club, its supporters and players and how it acquired the reputation of great Cup Giant-Killers.

The book is written primarily for football supporters – Tranmere fans interested in the origins of the name and the links with the Vikings, and the very many Scandinavian supporters who come to Tranmere and Liverpool games. We hope you enjoy reading about the connections.

Tranmere - Tranmæl

Tranmere is the same as Tranmæl in Norway. In modern Norway and Denmark cranebirds/herons are known as *trane* and they are known as *trana* in Sweden. Besides Tranmæl, the place names *Tranebjerg, Tranbjerg* and *Tranby* are common across Scandinavia. In addition, we find the word appearing in the name Martin Tranmæl (1879-1967), former leader of the Norwegian Labour/Socaliast movement.

Viking settlers led by Ingimund arrive on Wirral © Chris Collingwood.

Heron walking majestically on the beach at the bottom of a sandhill. Courtesy of Nicole St. Aubin.

Top: Tranmere in Wirral. Bottom: Tranmæl in Trøndelag, Norway. Photo: Stein Thue.

Tranmere Rovers FC. Photo: Per Anders Todal.

Tranny the Heron at Richmond Bridge.

Martin Tranmæl

Tranmæl was born in 1879 in the South Trøndelag (Trondheim) region of Norway. He worked as a painter and then as a journalist for the Trondheim newspaper *Ny Tid* "New Time", becoming active in the growing Norwegian Labour/Socialist movement. He became a member of the Social Democrat Labour Party's national executive and central committees and editor of the party's magazine, which developed into the modern *Dagsavisen* "The Day's News". Tranmæl's role in the party was so major that it was sometimes described as the "Tranmæl Party". Although he is best known as a champion for workers rights, he also was a pivotal member of the Nobel Peace Prize Committee. Although he died in 1967 he is still remembered as one of Norway's most well respected politicians.

Martin Tranmæl and (right) where he was allegedly at his best — on the soap box. Photograph: Oslo Museum — Creative Commons 3.0 license.

How did the Norsemen get to Wirral?

To answer this question we need to consider the migrations of peoples into the British Isles from Scandinavia over a millennium ago. Whereas the Danish invasions of Britain were directed mainly across the North Sea, and then by rivers such as the Humber, Ouse and Trent – and with very much military conquest in mind – by contrast the main route of the Norwegians or "Norsemen" into the British Isles was via the Scottish Isles and down the Irish Sea, establishing colonies in the Shetlands, Orkneys, Hebrides and the Isle of Man *en route* to Dublin where they established a major trading centre in the 9th Century. Their intentions were to some extent more peaceful, combining adventure and bravado with a need to settle in new lands after being forced out of Norway through either overcrowding or through expulsion after refusal to accept King Harald Hårfagre as the overall King of Norway.

Harald Hårfagre

The causes of what we now know as the Viking Age are still a matter of debate but the consensus of opinion appears to be that it was due to a combination of several factors[1]. One of these was a great thirst for adventure from young Scandinavian men: one of the famous sagas, for example, reports how the young Icelander Egil Skallagrímsson dreamt of becoming a Viking[2]. According to the Sagas Egil certainly achieved this and in later life he fought on the winning side at the *Battle of Brunanburh* in AD 937, considered by most scholars to have taken place on Wirral[3]. This desire was probably reinforced by an overcrowding of many of those parts of Scandinavia able to sustain a population – an increasing scarcity of good farming land and coastal areas in which to fish.

The second factor was the availability of the means to achieve this – the development of the longboat or longship – a superb piece of craftsmanship emanating from Scandinavia. The longboat evolved from a clinker-built

---

1. G. Jones (2001) *A History of the Vikings (2nd edition)*. Oxford University Press.
2. S. Sturluson, Egil's Saga, in Ö. Thorsson, (editor) and B. Scudder B. (2001) *The Sagas of the Icelanders*, Penguin Books, New York.
3. M. Livingston, Editor (2011) *Brunanburh: A Casebook*. Exeter University Press.

(overlapping planks) craft without a sail – an early example, dated to around AD 400, was found at Nydam on the Jutland peninsula[4]. Once a strong keel – which held the sail – became available, the potential to explore lands afar became a reality. Several examples have been discovered, the most notable being the Oseberg and Gokstad ships now displayed at the Oslo Ship Museum in Bygdøy, and also some of the Skuldelev ships at Roskilde. Another important factor behind the Viking Age was the changing political climate in Norway and in particular the emergence of a great hulking figure from the latter part of the 9th Century who united the many Norwegian kingdoms under one control – his own. That man was Harald Hårfagre. According to sources such as *Heimskringla*[5] written by Snorri Sturluson sometime between 1223 and 1225 and *Egil's Saga* – also considered by scholars to have been written by the same author - Harald Hårfagre was responsible for uniting the several independent kingdoms under one throne:

"Haraldr, son Hálfdanar svarta, hafði tekit arf eptir föður sinn; hann hafði þess heit strength, at láta eigi skera hár sitt né kemba, fyrr en hann væri einvaldskonungr yfir Noregi"

which translates as "Harald, son of Hálfdan the Black, had succeeded his father; he had made a solemn vow neither to cut nor comb his hair until he was king of all Norway". According to the saga unification of Norway was a requirement of the Hordaland (Harding) woman *Gyda* before she would agree to marry him. The subduing of the Norwegian kingdoms by Harald was subsequently achieved by a series of battles and treaties, culminating in one great battle at Hafrsfjordur (now Havsfjord, just west of Stavanger) which took place around the year AD 890: according to *Heimskringla*: "after this battle King Harald met no opposition in Norway for all his worst enemies had fallen. But some – and they were a great number, fled out of the country and thereby great uninhabited districts were peopled".

---

4. M. Magnusson (2000) *The Vikings*. Tempus Publishing, Stroud, page 18.
5. S. Sturluson, in P. Foote (editor) and P. Laing (translator) (1961) Heimskringla, *Everyman's Library*, J.M. Dent & Sons, London.

Dublin

Well before the battle of Hafrsfjordur, Vikings were already marauding down the Irish Sea. In or around the year AD 841 they discovered an ideal base for their operations at an inlet along a river on the east coast of Ireland – this was the River Liffey and the inlet became known as the "Black Pool" – dyf-lin or Dublin. The inlet was ideal for mooring and repairing their ships and was also located near a monastery which the Vikings would have found easy pickings to plunder. Dublin became an area of intense Viking settlement particularly around the area known as Wood Quay where there have been extensive excavations of the former Viking town. Dublin provided the main base for their operations in the Irish Sea and also a major centre for trade. However, at the beginning of the 10th Century that all changed.

Model of Harald Hårfagre and his wife Gyda at the Nordvegen Historical Centre, Karmøy, Haugesund.

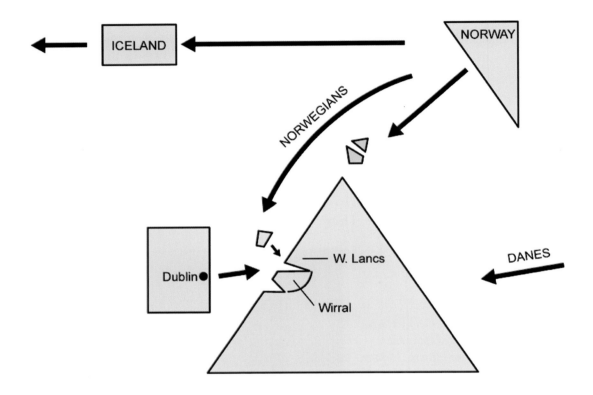

The exodus from Denmark and Norway. The major settlements of Wirral would have occurred after AD 902 with the expulsions from Ireland but scholars believe that large numbers would have also come from the Isle of Man and the Scottish Isles and even from Norway and Iceland. Drawing by John Harding.

Chapter 2
THE ARRIVAL OF THE VIKINGS: INGIMUND'S STORY

In this Chapter we present an extract from a set of old Irish annals called the "Three Fragments" which describe the arrival of the first group of Norwegians led by Ingimund (called Hingamund by the annalist) into the Wirral at the start of the 10th Century. These were people who had attempted to settle first in Ireland – probably Dublin - but were driven out by Caerbhall, leader of the Leinster Irish. Then they tried to gain a foothold in Anglesey – were driven out of there too – then received permission from "Edelfrida, queen of the Saxons" (Æthelflæd, daughter of Alfred the Great) to settle in Wirral, landing probably at the old trading port of *Melr* -Meols or *Vestri Kirkubyr* -West Kirby, or possibly even Wallasey Pool (now Wallasey Docks).

The transcripts have themselves had a fascinating history. Although the original vellum[6] manuscript last seen in the 16th Century had been lost, a copy of a copy eventually found its way to an Irish scholar - John O'Donovan - who edited and published the story with the Irish Archaeological and Celtic Society in 1860[7].

Since then the story has been under the scrutiny of scholars worldwide, but the general consensus is that the essence of the Ingimund story is true as it fits in with all the other historical evidence from the time. It also fits with all the place name evidence – Danish scholar J.J.A. Worsaee[8] earlier in 1851 had noted the existence of a large concentration of place names of Scandinavian origin in Wirral.

---

6. Parchment made from calfskin.

7. J. O'Donovan (1860) Annals of Ireland, Three Fragments, *Irish Archaeological and Celtic Society*, pages 227-237.

8. J.J.A. Worsaae (1851) *Minder om Danske og Nordmændene i England, Skotland og Irland,* Copenhagen - published in English in 1852 as *An Account of the Danes and Norwegians in England, Scotland and Ireland,* London.

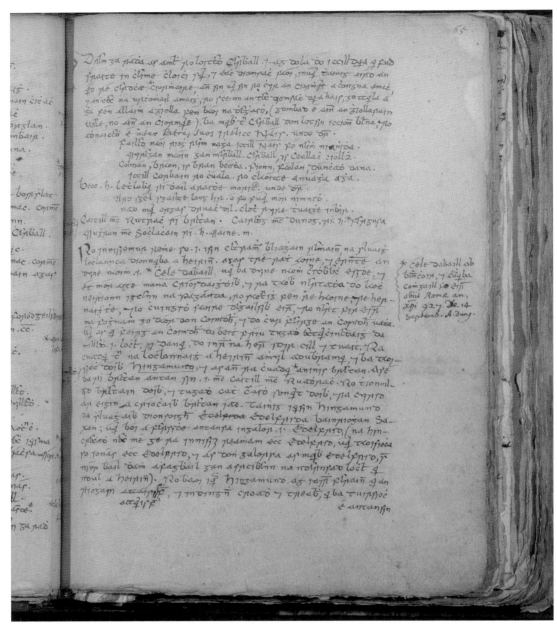

A 16th Century copy of the ancient Irish Annals known as the 'Three Fragments' containing Ingimund's Story. The names of the holy man Cele Dabhaill, the Norse leader Ingimund, and the king and queen of the Anglo-Saxons, Æthelred and Æthelflæd are underlined by the writer. This copy is presently at the Royal Library of Belgium.

Chapter 3
THE VIKING SETTLEMENTS

There are over 600 place names in Wirral with Norse or Norse-Irish roots, the majority being concentrated in the northern part of the peninsula. In the words of BBC Historian Michael Wood[13] the whole area is stuffed full of Viking names. These names are classed as "major names" – those that give their names to settlements, and "minor" names, from field, track and river names or certain topological features. One example, just 15 minutes walk from Tranmere Rovers FC is *The Arno*, off Storeton Road, which is thought to derive from Old Norse *Arni's haug* – a burial mound for the Norse settler *Arni*, now partly built on.

Other interesting examples are Heskeths, between Woodlands Road and Thingwall Road at Irby (one of two Heskeths in Wirral) – which comes from Old Norse *hesta skeið* – "horse race track", and The Breck at Wallasey (from Old Norse *brekka* – slope on a hillside), which has the fascinating rock formerly known as Clynsse, from Old Norse *klint* – projecting rock. There is also for example Svartskerre (now Fort Perch rock) at New Brighton, from Old Norse *svart sker* "black rock" and Tanskey Rocks at West Kirby, from Old Norse *tonn sker* "tooth skerry". The boundary of the main settlement area is Raby which comes from Old Norse "*rá-býr,* "village/farmstead at a boundary", with Tranmere well inside.

A complete list of minor names and their Ordnance Survey coordinates is given in the companion book *Ingimund's Saga*. Apart from the brief pictorial tour which follows from around Wirral and a consideration of major names we will just focus on those in Tranmere.

---

13. In '*The Great British Story: A People's History*' (2012): For links to this see www.nottingham.ac.uk/-sczsteve

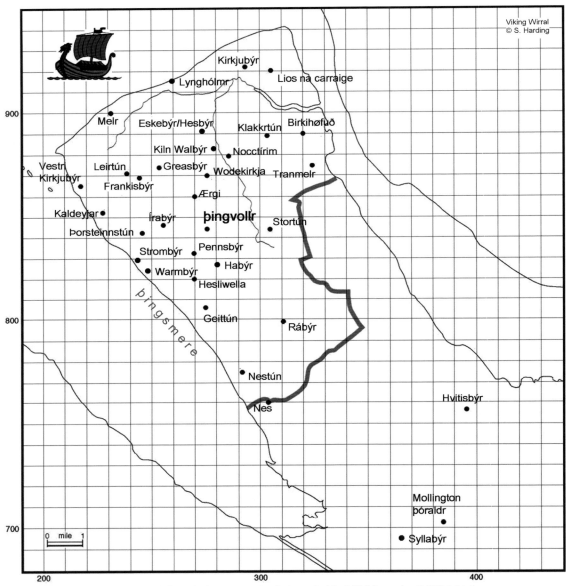

Viking Wirral – map of major Wirral place names in their probable Old Norse (or Old Irish) forms - can you identify these with their modern forms? Norse þ is pronounced "Th". For an explanation of Þingsmere, the Thing's mere" see Chapter 5. The line marks the probable boundary of the original Norse settlements.

Top - The Arno – Arni's haug today, seen from Storeton Road.
Bottom - Heskeths at Irby, seen from the bottom of Woodlands Road, near Arrowe Brook.
Imagine the sound of the hooves as the Vikings raced their horses!

Top: Piladall (Willow tree valley – Old Norse pill – Willow tree - and dalr - valley) on the edge of Raby. The arrow marks a present-day Willow tree. Bottom: The Barnston Gill. The dip down to the Fender valley at the end of Gills Lane.

Top: The "Klint" rock at the Wallasey Breck, at the end of Millthwaite Road. Photograph taken before the "Grafitti" era. Courtesy Wallasey Central Reference Library. Bottom: Svartskerre – the waves lash out at the Black Rock and the 19th Century fort built on it. Photograph: Bob Warwick.

Top: Tanskey Rocks (Old Norse tonn –sker "tooth skerry") at West Kirby, with some trani amongst the birdlife in the foreground and the Welsh hills in the distance. Bottom: Helsby Hill, from the M56 Motorway. The first glimpse of "Viking" Wirral for travellers coming to a Tranmere Rovers match.

Viking Wirral that "Away" supporters driving in along the M56 motorway to a Tranmere Rovers game see.

The place names Irby, Noctorum and Liscard all indicate a significant Irish presence in Ingimund's Wirral. Indeed it is highly likely that many of the Norsemen arriving from Ireland had Irish wives, and this may account for the presence of Christian Viking Churches such as St. Bridget's – which gives its name to West Kirby. Another Church with strong Norse-Irish roots is the Church of St. Mary and St. Helen in Neston. Both St. Bridgets and St. Mary and St. Helen, as well as St. Barnabas in Bromborough have some remarkable examples of Irish-Norse archaeology which we will discuss in Chapter 6. Down the road at Chester is the Church of St. Olave, dedicated to the Patron Saint of Norway St. Olav Haraldsson[15] the "Viking Saint" who died at the Battle of Stikklestad in 1030.

St. Olav, patron saint of Norway: Sculpture at Nidaros Cathedral, Trondheim. Courtesy of Stein Thue.

15. See links on www.nottingham.ac.uk/~sczsteve

Two Wirral Churches with strong Viking connections: Top St. Bridget's at West Kirby and bottom: St. Mary and St. Helen at Neston — both have some fascinating examples of hiberno-Norse archaeology.

Another significant place is **DENHALL** (now Denhall Farm), not marked on our map of Viking Age Wirral but *listed in 19th Century Tithe Maps as Denhall Field (Ordnance Survey* SJ320747) and *Denhall Hay* (SJ303749): Denhall is just south of Ness along the Dee coast. The name derives from *Danir-waella* – (Old Norse *Danir*) - the "Spring of the Danes". The Story of Ingimund reports that there were Danes in Ingimund's Wirral. They may have come over from Ireland with him or have already been here. The Anglo-Saxon Chronicle reports Danes raiding in Chester some ten years previous, maybe a group of them had stayed and settled.

Minor place names in Tranmere

Minor names on Wirral named after field, track and other features are too numerous to list here so we will just give those in Tranmere[16]. Rather than use postcodes we have given the Ordnance Survey co-ordinates to help the enthusiast find them (using the A-Z or Land Ranger maps for example, or Ordnance Survey on-line finders such as http://sewhgpgc.co.uk/xc/os2.php).

HINDERTON
SJ324880. *Hindri-tún* "Back of the farmstead". From Old Norse *hindri* (back, rear), and *tún* (farmstead). At the end of what is now Hinderton Close.

HINDERTON LANE
From SJ320881 to SJ325877. Now Hinderton Road.

ASKER DALE
SJ327877 *askr-dalr* "Ash-tree valley". From Old Norse *askr* (ash) and *dalr* (valley). Now an industrial area between Campbeltown Road and New Chester Road. The nearest trees are on the opposite side of either road.

---

16. See J. McNeal. Dodgson (1972) *The Place Names of Cheshire Part IV*, English Place Name Society Volume 47, Cambridge University Press.

INTAKE

SJ316877 "Enclosure". From Old Norse *inntak*. Now part of a housing estate off Maybank Road.

SLACK FIELD

SJ331868 "Field at the hollow". From Old Norse *slakki* (a hollow or cut-through). Now a communal area, partly wooded, between Bedford Place and Bedford Road.

KIRKS SLACKS

SJ320865 *kirkja-slakki* "Hollow near the church". From Old Norse *kirkja* (church) and *slakki* (hollow).

KIRKET HAY

SJ324860 "The enclosure by the church". From Old Norse *kirkja*.

RAKE HAY

SJ318871 "Enclosure by the lane". From Old Norse *rák*. Now built on with houses off Stewart Road. Not far from the Tranmere "Home Brew" Centre.

FAR STORETON FIELD, NEAR STORETON FIELD

SJ315859 and SJ316861 from Old Norse *storr* (great) and *tún* (farmstead). On the edge of what is now Storeton, between Mount Road and Raby Grove.

RAYNILDES POOL (1323)

From SJ330882 to SJ322885 "Ragnhildr's Pool" from an Old Norse female personal name *Ragnhildr*. Ragnhildr's Pool was lost in the construction of the docks and Cammell Laird shipyard, with the drained stream above it now the site of Dingle Road and the Valley Lodge in Devonshire Park.

GUNNEL POOL (1800)

SJ330872 "Gunnhildr's Pool" from another Old Norse female personal name Gunnhildr. Gunnhildr's Pool, recorded in 1529 as Gonnille Pool, represents another creak in from the Mersey between what is now St. Pauls Road and the oil terminal.

Top: Ragnhildr's Pool is now part of Cammell Laird Shipyard, off Campbeltown Road. Bottom: Gunnhildr's Pool is now part of the Tranmere Oil Terminal.

Minor names tell us of a persistence of a Norse dialect

For a full list of minor names of Norse origin the interested reader is referred to *Ingimund's Saga*, also from Countyvise.   Besides elements like *ærgi, brekka, slakki* and *gil*, we find elements like *rák* (lane), *thveit* (thwaite - clearing), *kjarr* (carr – marsh), *skali* (hut) and *holm* are common.

There are about 50 examples of carrs and about 25 examples of holms - most of the carrs and holms are situated around the Rivers Birket and Fender. There are also something like 100 examples of rakes in Wirral, which led someone to jokingly say that Wirral has "more rakes than BBC Gardener Alan Titchmarsh and more carrs than BBC Top Gear presenter Jeremy Clarkson"!

Most minor names cannot be traced right back to the Viking settlement period, as field names and tracks names could change depending on the local farmer or landowner at that time. But what these elements do tell us is the persistence of Norse words in the local Wirral dialect through the centuries.

Sir Gawain and the Green Knight

Further evidence of the persistence of a Scandinavian dialect comes from an unlikely source – the famous 14th Century poem *Sir Gawain and the Green Knight*, which points to the survival from the settlement period of a large number of dialect words of Norse origin. The general setting of the poem is across the northern Anglo-Welsh borderlands and some of the action takes place in Wirral.

The start of the poem tells of how a mysterious Green Knight arrives at the Court of Arthur and asks if anyone is brave enough to take part in a duel. Arthur regards the rules of the contest proposed by the Knight as absurd: the challenger is to take the first blow but the Green Knight must be allowed to take the second strike one year on. Sir Gawain volunteers himself and accepts the conditions. With the first blow the Green Knight loses his head but to everyone's astonishment he picks it up and rides away reminding Gawain of the condition he has agreed to, and to meet him at a place known as the Green Chapel after one year and a day. At the appropriate time Gawain keeps his word and goes in search of the Green Chapel. The journey – part of which is through Wirral - is long, arduous and dangerous and he eventually stops at a castle where a Sir Bercilak or *Bertilak* welcomes him to stay. He passes a test of faith – in the form of Bercilak's wife who tries to seduce him – and then Bercilak points him in the direction of the Green Chapel, which happens to be not far away. The Green Knight is found, Gawain offers himself for receiving the second strike, but it is only a glancing blow: the Green Man spares Gawain for being a man of his word, then reveals himself to be Sir Bercilak. Gawain then returns to Camelot[17].

Identity of the Sir Gawain poet

Although the identity of the poet is unknown, a study of the language and dialect of the poem has led a number of experts to believe that he/she may have come from somewhere in Wirral or not far away (especially as part of the action takes place there), and some have linked the authorship of the story with the Knight of the Garter Sir John Stanley (1345-1413) of Storeton Hall – not far from Tranmere Rovers FC - either as the patron of the poet or the poet himself[18]. We probably will never know for sure. Stanley was a Knight who served both King Richard II and King Henry III.

From a Viking perspective, the incorporation of a large number of Norse dialect words makes the language of the poem very different from Chaucer's Canterbury Tales – written at around the same time - indicating how "Norse" 14th Century Tranmere and Wirral must have still been.

---

17. There are many books on the Green Knight and its translation. See for example W.R.J. Barron (1998) *Sir Gawain and the Green Knight*, Manchester University Press and a children's version is by Selina Hastings (1991) *Sir Gawain and the Green Knight*, Walker Books Ltd., London.

18. E. Wilson (1979) Sir Gawain and the Green Knight and the Stanley Family of Stanley, Storeton and Hooton, *The Review of English Studies*, volume 30, pages 308-316.

To give an impression, 40 of these dialect words from the poem are listed as follows, together with their meaning and Old Norse root word. Some experts believe there are up to 450.

astyt: means "at once, straight away" (Old Norse *títt*)

ay: always, ever (Old Norse *ei*)

bole: tree-trunk (Old Norse *bolr*)

bonk: bank, hill, slope (Old Norse *banki*)

boun: ready; dressed (Old Norse *búinn*)

busk: get ready; dress (Old Norse *búask*)

cros: cross (Old Norse *kross*)

derf: stout (Old Norse *djarfr*)

dreped: killed (Old Norse *drepa*)

felle: mountain (Old Norse *fjall, fell*)

fro: from (Old Norse *frá*)

gate: road (Old Norse *gata*)

gayn: advantage, a good thing (Old Norse *gegn*)

gaynly: fitly, rightly (Old Norse *gegn*)

gef: gave (Old Norse *gefa, gaf*)

glent: glance (Old Norse *glenta* 'to glance')

hendelayk: courtliness (Old Norse *leikr*)

karp: talk (Old Norse *karpa* 'boast')

kest: to cast (Old Norse *kasta*)

lemed: shone (Old Norse *ljóma*)

meekly: meekly (Old Norse *mjúkliga*)

menskful: gracious; term of address - lady (Old Norse *mennskr* 'human')

myre: mire, swamp (Old Norse *mýrr*)

raged: ragged (Old Norse *røggvaðr or raggaðr*)

rapes: to hasten, hurry (Old Norse *hrapa*)

same, samen: together (Old Norse *saman*)

semly: seemly (Old Norse *sæmiligr*)

sere: separate; several (Old Norse *sér*)

skere: pure (Old Norse *skærr*)

skyl: reason (Old Norse *skil*)

stor: strong, severe (Old Norse *stórr*)

tok: took, **tan**: taken (Old Norse *taka, tók, tekinn*)

tore: hard, difficult (Old Norse *tórr*)

trayst: certain, sure (Old Norse *treistr, treista* 'trusted', 'trust')

tyl: until (Old Norse *til*)

þay: they (Old Norse *þeir*)

vmbe: to be surrounded (Old Norse *umb*)

wale: to choose, **waled**: chosen (Old Norse *velja, valdi*)

won, wone: dwelling (Old Norse *ván* 'hope')

More of these words can be found in *Viking Mersey*[19] and *Vikingblod*[20]. Stanley, besides being an ancestor of the Earls of Derby, is also the Great (x19) Grandfather of the author of this book[21].

---

19. S.E. Harding (2002) *Viking Mersey*, Countyvise, Birkenhead UK.
20. S.E. Harding and S. Vaagan (2011) *Vikingblod: spor av vikinger i Nordvest-England,* Genesis Forlag, Oslo.
21. http://www.nottingham.ac.uk/~sczsteve/Stanley_Wharton_line.htm

14th Century Scribe
(Courtesy of Wikipedia Commons)

Opposite, top: The Green Knight at the Court of Arthur (Courtesy of Juan Wijngaard).
Opposite, bottom: Storeton Hall. Parts of the Hall still remain from the 14th Century – when Sir John Stanley, believed to be the Patron of the Sir Gawain and Green Knight poet, lived here. Stanley was Knight of the Garter and also Master Forester of Wirral.

Rent Books

This persistence of a Norse dialect is also reinforced by records from people's rent books at the time. We find in rental records that in the year 1398 for the village of Great Sutton in Wirral an *Agnes Hondesdoghter* & a *Johanne Hondesdoghter* rented a cottage each for 2 shilling. These records also register in the same village that a certain *Richard Hondesson* rented two bovates[22] for 20 shilling and three acres for 4 shilling.

Nearby, a similar rental agreement for Childer Thornton, also in Wirral records that *Mabilla Raynaldesdoghter* rented a cottage at 1 shilling. This is rather remarkable in that the "daughters of Hondes", the "son of Hondes" and the "daughter of Raynald" show that in Wirral as late as the turn of the 15th Century Scandinavian customs were still being practised[23]. To put this in its context it was almost contemporary with Henry V fighting at Agincourt and not long before Richard III was losing his crown at Bosworth Field.

Intriguingly, also in nearby Whitby, one of the fields is recorded in 1440 as *Rawnuesfeld*, which probably preserves the same root name *Ragnaldr* (not necessarily the same man) as the father of Mabilla.

Although the influence of those early Scandinavian settlers had persisted through the centuries, by the 15th Century all knowledge of the settlement period would have been forgotten about. It would not be until the end of the 18th Century and the dawn of the 19th Century and the growth of the port of Liverpool and its environs when that would change. A powerful middle class was starting to emerge, with a strong desire to learn about the past. This was the start of the "Romantic" period and a fascination with things gone by was sometimes coloured with a capacity to speculate. It is the Victorians for example who propagated the notion that Vikings wore horns on their helmets — they never did - and it was two particular local legends — one concerning the Norse god Thor and his association with a rock at Thurstaston Common — "Thor's stone", the other concerning the Danish

---

22. A bovate is a unit of land.

23. This form of naming children is identical to that still practised in Iceland – for example a recent President of Iceland was Vigdís Finnbogadóttir: the daughter of Finnbogi.

King Canute and his attempt to turn back the tide – which particularly captured their imagination[24]. It was the Victorians on Merseyside – including the scholar and artist W.G. Collingwood (one of his paintings is shown in Chapter 5) who helped rediscover the historical tradition of the settlement period. Nowadays many people on Wirral are aware of their Viking past.

William Gershom Collingwood (1854-1932) - Old Norse scholar of Merseyside origins: artist, folklorist, historian and archaeologist, who helped rescue the Vikings from obscurity.

24. See S.E. Harding (2002) *Viking Mersey*, Countyvise, Birkenhead, which puts these legends in their context. See also www.nottingham.ac.uk/-sczsteve

Tom and Matt Harding at Thor's Stone, Thurstaston wearing the modern uniform of a Wirral Viking – a Tranmere Rovers shirt. Like the Klint rock at the Wallasey Breck, Thor's Stone is a great rock to climb by youngsters and oldsters alike – and there are some great views from the top of Thurstaston Common, nearby.

Chapter 4
THE VIKING PEOPLE OF TRANMERE AND WIRRAL

The Viking Age women of Tranmere and Wirral

Besides Gunnhildr and Ragnhildr of Tranmere, other names of women appearing in place names and early Charters in Wirral are *Ingridr* of Capenhurst (last recorded in the place name Ingriessiche in 1340, which we think is somewhere between what is now Capenhurst Lane and Dunkirk Lane) and *Sigríðr* of Wallasey (recorded as Seurydzis Alfland in 1281 "Sigríðr's half-land", which we think is somewhere around what is now the St. Georges Road area in Wallasey Village). *Sigríðr* also appears in a list of pre-Domesday Moneyers as *Segrid*.

The appearance of these women in these records is a clear indication that in the Scandinavian community on 10th Century Wirral women played a significant role. Kristín Bragadóttir and Patrick J. Stevens in *Stefnumót við Íslenska Sagnahefð* (Living and Reliving the Icelandic Sagas), writing about women in Viking Society, and in particular Iceland, say the following:

'The women of the North played a fairly traditional role in society, as the rigours of childbearing and domestic life defined their lives. Nonetheless, Germanic law generally accorded Nordic women certain rights that most (other) European women did not enjoy. Pre-Christian Icelandic women could seek divorce as well as refuse betrothal. Icelandic women had also property rights; both the wife and mistress of Snorri Sturluson were women of considerable wealth'.

This situation may have been similar in Viking Age Wirral. The interested reader is referred to a contribution by Christina Lee in the 2014 book *In Search of Vikings* edited by S.E. Harding, D. Griffiths and E. Royles[25].

---

25. CRC Press, Boca Raton, Florida.

Top: Saga natt med mor (Saga-night with mother). Picture, courtesy of Jennifer McGlaughlin, www.jennifersillustrations.co.uk .
Bottom: Norsemen at Sea. Courtesy of Pocketbond Limited.

The Viking men of Wirral

We've already heard about Ingimund. But the names of the many men who were present in Wirral's Viking society are also recorded in place names, Charters and lists of landowners. Here are those appearing in the place names:

Arni

Gives his name to *The Arno* in the village of Oxton.

Fiðill

Gives his name to Fiddlestone in Burton Parish.

Grimr

Gives his name to Grymisgreue, last recorded in 1463 in Woodbank.

Karli

His name appears in Calthorpe in Bidston.

Ketill

Appears in Kettle Well Garden in Wallasey, and in Ketilspol "Ketill's Creek", last recorded in 1402 at Hooton in what is now Riveacre Park.

Ragnaldr

Gives his name to the field name Rawnuesfeld, last recorded in 1440 in Whitby. Instead of from Ragnaldr, the first element could also come from Old Norse *hrafn* "raven".

Steinkell

Appears in Steyncolesdale (which later became "Tinker's Dale"), last recorded in 1298 in Thurstaston.

Tóki

Gives his name to Tokesford, last recorded in 1397 in Wallasey - "Toki's crossing point" – see page 60.

Þórald

Gave his name to Mollington-Torrold, now Mollington.

Þórsteinn

Appears in Thurstaston.

Ufaldi

The name appears as Ufilys Brow in Saughall Massie and as Vfeldesgrene in Claughton in 1340, probably now part of Birkenhead Park.

Here are those men appearing in this extensive list of landowners[26]:

Arngrímr (recorded as Haregrim, Aregrim)
Arni (recorded as Erne, Erni)
Arnkell (Archil)
Ásgautr (Ansgot, Osgot)
Beollán (Belam)
Biornulfr (Bernulf)
Brunn (Brun)
Frani (Fran)
Gamall (Gamel)
Grímkell (Grinchel)
Grímr (Grim)
Gunningr (Gunninc)
Gunnarr (Gunner)
Gunnvor (Gunnor)
Guðleikr (Gotlac)
Hakon (Hacon, Hacun)
Hálfdan (Halden, Alden)
Hásteinn (Hasten)
Hrafn (Rauen)
Hrafnkell (Rauechel, Rauenchel, Rauecate)
Hrafnsvartr (Rauesuar, Rausue) – "the black raven"

---

26. From a list compiled by F.T. Wainwright (1942) North-West Mercia AD 871-924, Norse settlements around the Irish Sea. *Transactions of the Historic Society of Lancashire and Cheshire*, volume 94, pages 3-55. Reproduced in P. Cavill, S. Harding and J. Jesch (2000) *Wirral and its Viking Heritage*, English Place Name Society, Nottingham, UK, pages 19-42.

Hundingr (Hundingr, Hundin)
Hundólfr (Hundulf)
Karl, Karli (Carle)
Ketill (Chetel)
Kolbeinn (Colben)
Loðinn (Loten)
Morfari (Morfar)
Ormr (Orme)
Ragnaldr (Ragenal)
Steinkell (Steinchetel)
Steinn (Stein)
Steinólfr (Stenulf)
Tóki (Tochi)
Úlfkell (Ulchel, Ulchetel)
Úlfr (Ulf)
Vetriðr (Wintrelet)
Þioðólfr (Dedol, Dedou)
Þórðr (Toret, Toreth)

Farmers and fishermen

We know they were engaged in peaceful activities, from the numbers of arrowe field names. As we explained above arrowe (which has nothing to do with bow and arrow) is associated with a farming activity (from *erg* or *ærgi* – summer pastureland away from the farmhouse). Early forms on Wirral include Arwe (1240-1249) and Argh (1296). The practice of sending cattle away from the farmhouse thus saving the local pasture for winter fodder is known as "transhumance" and is still practised in modern Norway (see Chapter 1 by J. Jesch in *Wirral and its Viking Heritage*[27]). The preponderance of many field names in the locality bearing the Arrowe element, as recorded in the 19th Century tithe maps, suggests this practice was followed in Wirral until at least 150 years ago: Arrowe Brook & Arrowe Brook House, Arrowe Hill, Arrowe Bridge, Youd's & Bennet's Arrowe, Browns Arrowe, Bithels Arrowe, Harrisons Arrowe, Whartons Arrowe, Widings Arrowe.

---

27. P. Cavill, S.E. Harding and J. Jesch (2000) *Wirral and its Viking Heritage*, English Place-Name Society, Nottingham.

The settlers would have also taken advantage of the large proportion of coastal land and would have been expert fishermen. *Le Skereyorde* recorded in 1412 in Bromborough (and located probably near the mouth of the Dibbin) means "Fish trap at the skerry" from Old Norse *sker* "skerry".

Top: Skirmish between new Scandinavian arrivals into Wirral and Anglo-Saxons from Chester. Re-enactment by the Wirhalh Skip-Felag at Arrowe Park. Photo: Pip Shedden
Bottom: Norseman from the Wirhalh Skip-Felag stands guard by a stall at the Wirral Show, Wallasey.

Chapter 5
THE VIKING ASSEMBLY – THE THING

The existence of the community's Thing at Thingwall ('Assembly field') – one of only two definite Thingwall place-names in England – attests to the Scandinavians being the dominant population. Motorists driving through Wirral may have noticed a set of informative dual-language road signs denoting the origin of the name and the link with the Norse Assembly. Two of the old Thingwall signposts had "gone missing" and I had suggested to Wirral Council that they might replace them with the dual-language signs. Working with them, local Councilllor Don McCubbin and Mr. Roy Fisher of the Irby, Thursaston and Pensby Amenity Society we were able to replace all four road signs denoting the entry into Thingwall thanks to the generosity of United Facilities who funded the work[28].

The existence of a Thingwall in Wirral demonstrates just how significant the peninsula was in the Viking Age – a Thingwall is the sign of autonomy, self-government … Scandinavian power. Unfortunately the Vikings didn't leave any records telling us where in Thingwall the Place of Assembly was. However we have a pretty good idea.

Cross Hill

Many Thing sites across Scandinavia have a Thing *brekka* (Old Norse for a slope/hill) on which the speaker could stand in order to make himself/herself heard. It seems that the location in Thingwall which would appear to have best fitted this description is Cross Hill (Old Norse - *kross*).

Here the Thing Assembly would have met once or twice a year to discuss matters of policy and law, and also in times of crisis. It would also have been a time to meet old friends, and Vikings from outside Wirral may well have visited.

---

28. See various links to newspaper articles and a radio and TV broadcast on www.nottingham.ac.uk/~sczsteve

Left: Signpost at Irby, full of Viking names.   Right: Signpost with a supporter wearing a Tranmere scarf on the A551 approach to Thingwall at Cross Hill.   The most likely site of the Thing is believed to be the right of the hedge across the road.

Left: Cross Hill.   Right: Drawing by C. Krohg of a meeting of the Thing Assembly.

Painting by Liverpudlian W. G. Collingwood of a meeting of the Thing Assembly at Thingvellir in Iceland. The Thingvatn (Thing water) can clearly be seen.

Other Thingwalls in Northern Europe

The settlements in Wirral spread to West Lancashire and there is another Thingwall near Knotty Ash. Other examples in the British Isles include Tynwald in the Isle of Man, Dingwall in north-east Scotland, Tinwald in south-west Scotland and Tingwall in the Shetlands. There are many others in Scandinavia and Iceland including Tingvoll near Molde in Norway. The modern Norwegian Parliament is the "Storting" which literally means the "big Thing".

The most well-known is Thingvellir at Almannagja, Iceland. Some Thing sites also have a stretch of water associated with them. In Iceland the Thing site at Thingvellir is near *Þingvatn* "Thing water". In 2004 I suggested that the place Dingesmere in the Anglo Saxon poem *The Battle of Brunanburh* referred to the Things mere – the mere or waterway associated with the *Thing*. Nobody was quite sure where this famous battle in year AD 937 - which according to some reports had Vikings fighting on both sides - may have taken place, although Brunanburh was the old name of Bromborough (see the map from 1724 on page 23) and most scholars had already a good idea that the battle took place on Wirral. Working with colleagues we then presented evidence that either Wirral's coastal Dee region, or the region around Meols, was the site of Wirral's "Thingsmere" (the wetland/waterway of the Thing) in the poem, reinforcing the argument for a Wirral location of the battle[29].

Dee coastline at Heswall Point near Sheldrakes Restaurant.

29. www.nottingham.ac.uk/ncmh/dna/Brunanburh.htm

Chapter 6
THE LEGACY OF THE VIKINGS: GENES, ARCHAEOLOGY, A WALK, A VIKING NAVY – AND TRANMERE ROVERS

Legacy of the Vikings remains in the genes of old Wirral families

Although the last meeting of the Thing would have been a millennium ago, a recent genetic survey of Wirral and neighbouring West Lancashire has shown that the legacy of those people who once met there remains even today.

Hair and eye colour have traditionally been used as traits of Scandinavian ancestry – a very high proportion of people from the Baltic Sea region have fair hair and light eyes. Although the genetic basis behind these traits is quite complex it is now quite well understood.

Another trait linked with Scandinavia is a condition of the hand known as Dupuytren's contracture: the onset of the condition is a tightening of the elastic tissue in the palm of the hand causing difficulty in flexing the 4th and 5th fingers. A recent Mayor of Wirral was found to have this condition in both hands! However up until recently much of the genetic research has focused on the small part of our DNA which is passed directly down the male line without change: this is known as Y-chromosomal DNA.

The Genetic Survey of Wirral and West Lancashire (2002-2008) – led by the University of Leicester (the birthplace of Forensic Genetics) and the University of Nottingham - looked at Y-DNA distributions amongst male volunteers who had surnames that were present in Wirral 1600 or before. This proved possible because of King Henry VIII's great diligence in recording all those households on Wirral paying taxes in 1542! Other Medieval lists included Alehouse records and criminal records. For example Thomas Harding and Robert Poole of Neston were accused of damaging hedges and killing someone's dog in 1348…. and fortunately found to be not guilty (a good decision!).

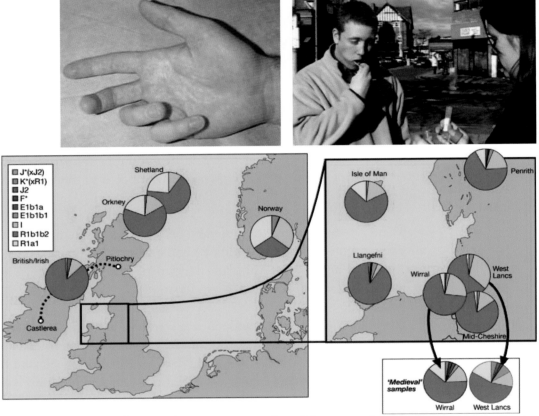

Top left: Dupuytren's contracture, a genetic condition connected with the Vikings. Photo: Courtesy Dr. Jeff Whiting, Saint Louis University School of Medicine.

Top right: Taking a DNA sample (cheek swab) from a volunteer at West Kirby.

Bottom: Distribution of Y-DNA types (listed in the box). These types refer to patterns of DNA on the male Y-chromosome which are passed down along the male line (like surnames) without change. For example Tranmere fan Rich Harding's chromosome belongs to the orange sector, "K*(xR1)" in the pie chart for 'Medieval' Wirral. The greater the "pie slice" the greater the proportion of people with that type. From detailed statistical analysis of this data it is possible to assess the extent of Scandinavian ancestry in the DNA admixture of a region[30]. 'Medieval' samples are the data-sets based on people with surnames present in an area before 1600.

30. G.R. Bowden, P. Balaresque, T.E. King, Z. Hansen, A.C. Lee, G. Pergl-Wilson, E. Hurley, S.J. Roberts, P. Waite, J. Jesch, A.L. Jones, M.G. Thomas, S.E. Harding and M.A. Jobling (2008) Excavating past population structures by surname-based sampling: the genetic legacy of the Vikings in North West England. *Molecular Biology and Evolution* volume 25, pages 301-309.

catalogued[35] and include coins, Hiberno-Norse pins, brooches, a drinking horn and what appear to be weapons from a possible pagan burial. Evidence has been presented of the remains of an elliptically shaped Viking house off Mill Lane at Irby[39], and a further Viking House off Dig Lane in Lingham/ Moreton. Amongst other impressive evidence for the Viking settlements are remains of Viking crosses at West Kirby and Hilbre, at Woodchurch and at St. Barnabas Church in Bromborough[40].

At the Church of St. Mary and St. Helen at Neston there are seven fragments belonging to at least three Hiberno-Norse crosses, with fascinating imagery including the touching scene of a Viking couple embracing[41] and not far away in Ness a silver ingot from the Viking Age was discovered[42].

Viking blood and genes are still very much alive within current generations and this is manifested both in a major Viking heritage walk which takes place in Wirral every year and the setting up of Wirral's own 'Viking Navy'.

St. Olav's Day walk

Since 2008, every July 29th – St. Olav's Day – or thereabouts, hordes of enthusiasts including many Tranmere supporters have trudged the twenty or so miles between West Kirby, Wirral, via Thurstaston and Neston to St. Olave's Church. The walk, Wirral's own version of Norway's St Olav Pilgrimage from Oslo to Trondheim (approximately 400 miles) – commemorating the patron Saint of Norway and Scandinavia Olav Haraldsson, buried at Trondheim – was captured in Michael Wood's 2011 BBC series *The Great British Story*[43]. The walk starts at St. Bridgets Church

39. R.A. Philpott and M. Adams (2010) *Irby, Wirral: Excavations on a Late Prehistoric, Romano-British and Medieval Site*, 1987-1996.

40. J.D. Bu'Lock (1958) Pre-Norman crosses of West Cheshire and the Norse settlements around the Irish Sea. *Transactions of the Lancashire and Cheshire Antiquarian Society* volume 68, pages 1-11. Reproduced in P. Cavill, S. Harding and J. Jesch (2000) *Wirral and its Viking Heritage*, English Place Name Society, Nottingham, UK, pages 70-83.

41. R.H. White (2014) Figuring it out: Further work on the Neston cross fragments, Cheshire. In S.E. Harding, D. Griffiths and E. Royles *In Search of Vikings*, CRC Press, Boca Raton, USA, Chapter 12. See also the links in www.nottingham.ac.uk/-sczsteve

42. S. Bean (2000) Silver ingot from Ness, Wirral. In P. Cavill, S. Harding and J. Jesch *Wirral and its Viking Heritage*, English Place Name Society, Nottingham, UK, pages 17-18.

West Kirby – with the famous Viking hogback tombstone - then past many interesting Viking sites and settlements, including the former Stromby and Warmby sites and Thorstein's farmstead (Thurstaston) to the church of St. Mary and St. Helen, the site of the hiberno-Norse cross fragments and an impressive replica cross reconstruction.

The final part of the walk – to St. Olave's - takes place on a following day, or the following year depending on how lazy or energetic we are!

Wirral's Viking Navy

Wirral set up its latter-day 'Viking navy' to row the largest working Scandinavian longship reconstruction – the Draken Harald Hårfagre – at the end of its epic maiden international sailing voyage from Karmøy, Norway to Wirral in 2014. The Draken is 35 metres long and 8 metres wide. When not being sailed but rowed it has 25 pairs of oars with 2 persons to an oar. The vessel was modelled on the *Leidangr* series of sea-defence vessels used in the 11th-12th Centuries at the end of the Viking Age in Scandinavia.

The 'navy', comprised a 100-strong band of local enthusiasts expertly trained by the Liverpool Victoria Rowing Club at Wallasey Docks on the River Mersey. In June 2013 in preparation for the longship coming to Wirral this formidable group 'raided' the Karmøy Viking Festival, taking the opportunity to gain invaluable practice rowing the vessel.

Just over twelve months later it set off from Karmøy and arrived at the mouth of the River Mersey passing by Liverpool's Pier Head in front of thousands of awestruck spectators. It was then carefully manoeuvred into the East and West Floats at its destination - Wallasey Docks, Wirral – just a few minutes down the river from Tranmere. There it remained near Toki's crossing point (see page 43) receiving essential repairs (including a new mast) after its epic voyage. Members of the public then had the opportunity to climb on board and witness what a Viking ship would have looked like a millennium ago. Wirral's Viking Navy were then able to majestically row the vessel around the sheltered waters of Wallasey Docks before this historic vessel finally returned to Norway.

Celebrity supporters of Tranmere, David Dimbleby (left) photograph by Laurence Bouce and Paul O'Grady (right), photograph by Steve Punter. David Dimbleby – whose surname is of Scandinavian origins – is a well known BBC commentator and presenter of current affairs and political programmes including BBC's long running Question Time television series[45]. Paul O'Grady MBE is a well-known television and radio presenter, actor, writer and comedian. Reproduced courtesy of Wikimedia Commons.

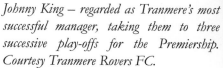

Johnny King – regarded as Tranmere's most successful manager, taking them to three successive play-offs for the Premiership. Courtesy Tranmere Rovers FC.

45. You can listen to his affection for Tranmere on a recording for BBC Radio Merseyside – see www.nottingham.ac.uk/-sczsteve for the link.

Thomas Myhre. Reproduced courtesy of Action Images.

He has appeared on many TV and Radio broadcasts and in 2011 King Harald V of Norway made him *Ridder 1. Klasse den Kongelige Norske Fortjenstorden* – Knight of the First Class of the Royal Norwegian Order of Merit.

Photo: Mike McCartney.

Vikings in Wirral web-site for schools: www.wirral-mbc.gov.uk/vikings/